I0438396

WORK ABILITIES

WORK ABILITIES

A Guide for Persons With

Disabilities Seeking Employment

Judith Thomas

Copyright © 2011 by Judith Thomas.

Library of Congress Control Number: 2011914724
ISBN: Hardcover   978-1-4653-5239-2
                   Softcover   978-1-4653-5238-5
                   Ebook   978-1-4653-5240-8

All rights reserved. No part of this book may be reproduced or transmitted
in any form or by any means, electronic or mechanical, including photocopying,
recording, or by any information storage and retrieval system,
without permission in writing from the copyright owner.

This book was printed in the United States of America.

To order additional copies of this book, contact:
Xlibris Corporation
1-888-795-4274
www.Xlibris.com
Orders@Xlibris.com
104010

"My belief is that both of the manuals Judith has written are long overdue 'missing pieces of the puzzle', for job seekers with disabilities, 'Workabilities' is a guide to who's who in the specialized employment services universe, it is a practical kit to navigating the sometimes confusing and hidden maze of services and supports available, a detailing of pitfalls to avoid and opportunities offered and finally and importantly, the guide instructs on how to keep hope alive and confidence high during a job search. In sum, 'Workabilities' is many things; and although time and persistence by job seekers may eventually uncover best ways to take advantage of all that the system has to offer, this guide offers a highly valuable 'shortcut', knitting together the best of best practices and approaches and presents all of these in a highly readable style."

Marianne Cooke,
Employment Support Consultant,
Link Up Employment Services for Persons with Disabilities,
Toronto, Canada

"I would like to dedicate this book to Raj Tribhuwan, who showed me that despite being blind, you can still accomplish great things."

J.T.

Introduction

This book is a no-nonsense manual to finding employment for persons with disabilities. It is a "How To" guide to navigate your way through the minefield of job search activities. It does not provide tons of examples of resumes and cover letters, because those are already out there. What it does do, is tell you where to look for them and tell you how to get yourself hooked up with a great job coach, training program or agency.

The material which follows is based on my many years of experience as a job coach and my own personal story. Being a very direct person, I have taken a plain-speaking approach to effective job searching. It contains very down to earth advice on how to steer through the twists and turns on the road to employment, or re-employment. I have not been afraid to tackle those "sticky" topics such as grieving, depression and bullying. You are free to take my advice, or leave it, as you choose. There might be a few hairpin bends included, so buckle up and here goes!

Chapter One

CAST OF CHARACTERS

In my wide spread use of the word JOB COACH, I am including Intake Coordinators, Workshop Facilitators, Employment Counsellors, Job developers, Program Managers, and Agency Representatives. In fact, anyone who offers you professional advice on your road to employment, or re-employment. This is because they may all have a hand in informing and instructing you along your route.

Coaching, counseling, or training can occur in person, either one on one, or in a group setting. It can be in your home, in a publicly recognized job search location, or it can be out at a venue such as a conference or job fair. Coaching can also be via e-mail, or even just over the telephone. My advice here is to listen as much as possible. You can then evaluate the advice, discard what you don't need and hang on to the stuff that you feel is relevant.

For those of you who are unsure of the above role names, here is a brief description:

Intake Coordinator

Generally this is your first point of contact with any agency or program that has more than one individual staff member. You can glean a lot from this person about the type of training program, or agency that you are dealing with. For your part, be honest with them in describing your wants, needs and limitations, so they are able to refer you on to the next step in your process. Generally speaking, these people hold a wealth of information for you to tap in to. Sometimes, not only on their own organizations, but often on other community agencies and organizations, who can also assist you. Another person, or persons, to access for information, are employment resource centre workers. They are often very knowledgeable about employment programs and community resources to help you get started.

Workshop Facilitator

This person manages the workshops on employment related topics. Look for ones who are very knowledgeable about their subjects and who do not have to stick to the script. Utilize the tools and techniques that you are provided with. The second final stage of learning is always to put in to practice what you learn. Check out their theories and see if they work well for you in actual practice.

Employment Counsellors

These are usually met with on an individual basis, for career advice and guidance. They can also work effectively with you, in a group setting, when you are undertaking testing or quizzes. Work closely with your job coach to figure out how your personality, values, and interests, play a key part in determining what type of role would be a good fit for you. There is also a lot of online testing available, some of it free and some with a fee associated.

Job Developers

These are the people that help you to connect directly with employers. Because they often meet with hiring managers and human resources specialists, their advice on preparing your best approach and interview skills, is usually very up to date and valuable. If they are able to give you a personal introduction to an employer, then that is pure gold and will save you many steps of elimination.

If you decide that you do not want to work with the particular employer that they have referred you to, then that is okay. At least, by meeting with them, you have had the opportunity to hear, directly from a prospective employer's mouth, what they look for in their candidates and in your documents. This could be invaluable to you when approaching other prospective employers.

Program Managers

Program managers are ultimately in charge of the training program you are enrolled in. They are there as back ups, in case you have questions regarding your personal situation, or interactions with their staff. Although usually seen as only a recourse if necessary, program managers have often started from the bottom up, and have a wealth of knowledge regarding employment. If they are ever invited to attend a workshop, or other function, I would pay close attention to their views. They can often add some perspective to your job search, as they can see the wider picture.

Agency Representatives

If you are working with an agency of any kind, you are working as part of a team. The agency rep has a mandate, either to an employer, or to a funder, to fill positions. So, they are on your side. They want you to be hired, as much as you want to be hired. If they have a fee for their services, then it is up to you to decide whether the end result will justify that fee.

Employment Consultants

Employment consultants are usually individuals who work independently from any agency, on a fee for service basis. In some cases, consultants are hired by organizations on a contract basis, to fill a niche role.

CHAPTER TWO

A JOB SEEKER'S VIEWPOINT

You have every right to be your own career manager.

Employment Specialists, like any other profession, are comprised of "The Good, The Bad and The Ugly". Believe me, I have met and worked with them all.

So here are a few tips and cautions:

1. Rights and Obligations.

You have the right to have an equal say in your job search process. For example:

Differing agencies have different styles of resume format. One agency I know of only allows their job coaches to prepare functional type resumes. That works great if you are a youth with little or no experience, are career changing, or have been out of the workforce for a long time. However, that may not be ideal for you.

Remember—Ultimately, your career is in your hands. If you are unhappy with their version of your resume, or their job search methods, you have the right not to accept their advice.

Warning—If your resume and methods aren't working, then perhaps you are on the wrong page yourself and your job coach is right.

Solution—Take a team approach. If your own resume and methods are working, then join a support group that fits your needs. My advice would always be to join a program, agency, job finding club, or work with an employment consultant. Statistics prove that those who belong to good support groups become more pro-active in their job search and find more meaningful employment sooner than those who try to go it alone. With any job coach, they need to do their part, and you need to do yours. Without both of you being proactive, it will take longer for you to become employed. This is especially true if you are hoping to career change. Regard all meetings with your job coach, or anyone else, as valuable networking and learning opportunities.

2. Bullying.

By far the majority of employment agencies and non-profit employment organizations truly care about their clients. Most of them hire well qualified, empathetic counselors, facilitators, intake coordinators and job developers. But, those "Ugly" ones we mentioned earlier are also out there.

Remember—If you are being coerced in to a position that you don't want, then you have the right to refuse. You may be looking for a temporary job to assist you financially, or you may be in the long haul search for meaningful employment. Either way, the choice is yours and there is no right or wrong concerning your needs and values.

Warning—There are some agencies and individuals who care more about their statistics and funding, profit margin, or personal reputation, than you as an individual. Many organizations have a "quota" to fill, in order to stay in business.

Solution—If you are unhappy with your job coach, their program, or the agency you are with, the solution is simple; ask them to close your file. Try an agency, or consultant, that you think is a better fit for your needs. Start by checking out their mandate, or vision statement. Does it sit well with your own values and beliefs?

3. Agency Hopping and Double Dipping.

This is when you deem that you have a better chance of success by signing up to several agencies and programs at one time. This may lead to confusion, especially if they are giving you conflicting advice. Employment specialists are as varied as other professionals in their material and their approach.

Warning—Signing up with more than one publicly funded agency is strictly not allowed. This is known in the trade as "double dipping," as you are accessing public funding twice over. You will soon be caught, as the Federal, Provincial and Municipally funded programs all require that you provide your social insurance number to the agency. This is their way of keeping tabs on how many training dollars you have run up in your job search.

It is also extremely unfair that you should be accepted to more than one program, when others may be sitting around on a waiting list.

Solution—Do your homework and chose an agency, individual coach, or program, that best fits your needs. Check out their mandates and talk to their staff. Ask your friends about their job searching experiences and which organizations helped them the most.

Warning regarding the solution—If you have been through several training programs, agencies and job coaches, then you need to seriously ask your self "WHY?"

The most common problem with someone who has run the gamut of agencies, is that they just aren't really committed to their job search. Some of you may find it hard to accept constructive criticism and some may just be the "L" word. Yes, you know it. It's a bad four letter word; lazy. Did I mention I'm very direct and don't pull any punches?

If you are not whole heartedly committed to your job search, then you are not ready to seek employment. There is no way to sugar coat this fact. There is a direct ratio between the amount of hours you spend on your job search process and how quickly you become employed. Not to mention the fact that you are more likely to find, and keep, meaningful employment, if you do your homework. Your homework is on yourself first, the labour market second, and on employers that meet your needs third.

4.   Expertise.

You may be an expert in your field, perhaps even hold a PHD, or two. But, that does not mean that you are an expert in job searching or career changing. Some of the worst resumes I have ever encountered have come to me from highly educated people.

Client A was a very gifted university student hoping to obtain a post with the university, for the summer. I was invited to her home and scanned her resume over a wonderful cup of tea. The tea was the only wonderful thing and ended up being sputtered across the table as I read in utter horror! At the top of her resume she had forgotten her e-mail address. But wait! It gets much worse than that! There was no skills, qualifications or profile section. There was no order discernable to her statements, including even a date order. It was merely a bland list of various student jobs she had held over the years. The top two listed were for babysitting. They included the name, address, and phone number of the children's parents. Yikes! So, I asked her why she felt she wanted this particular job. She went on to explain all the amazing things she had been involved with, through the university, mentoring students, cataloging in the library etc. Needless to say, we changed things up a bit with her documents and sure enough, she obtained her coveted placement.

5. The good and bad aspects of paying for service.

Paid Consultants and Agencies

Good Points:
1. Much more flexible hours and can receive service at a convenient time for you.
2. One-to-one coaching through transition
3. Can receive service at a mutually agreed location, over the telephone, or via the internet
4. Personalized and tailored guidance, rather than common and general information
5. Not locked in to a funder's mandate
6. Wide range of services offered, not just one training module
7. Long term coaching may be an option, rather than a specified time frame
8. Coaching while still in employment is also a possibility

Bad Points:
1. Fee not free
2. A disreputable person, or agency, could take your money and give poor results. I have seen many $300 resumes that were horrible.

Non Profits and Government Sponsored Services

Good Points:
1. No cost as your tax dollars pay for them
2. Often have a resource centre where you can review job search material without having to purchase it
3. Resource centre staff and intake coordinators are very knowledgeable about your community and what services are available for you
4. Group sessions may be more comfortable than individual coaching, for you

Bad Points:
1. Almost always inflexible in hours
2. Locked in to funder's mandates. So, government representatives may have input in what you require in the way of assisting your job search.
3. Agencies do not always hire the most professional, or well qualified, staff
4. Some programs are quota driven and treat you like a number

There may be other good and bad points to both that you have encountered through your own experiences. These are just a few that I have run into.

CHAPTER THREE

CAREER ADVISING AND TESTING

Without a direction, or career goal, you are not ready to begin job searching. How will you tailor your resume, if you don't know what type of work you are hoping to secure? How will you know which method, or methods, of job searching to employ, to get hired in that field? So, if you are unsure, this is your first priority. Work with an individual job coach, or in a group, to narrow down your focus. Start by asking yourself if you are looking for a temporary stop gap to fix your overdraft, or if you are looking for your true vocation in life. Remember to discuss with your coach, all the peripherals, especially your home situation, that affect your requirements. For example, if you have a partner that is committed to constant moving in their career, you may want to opt for shorter, contract positions.

This is an especially important phase if you are career changing.

Goals

Make sure your goals are realistic ones. You need to have the education and ability to apply for certain positions. If your goals are very big ones, and seem very hard to reach, then you need to chunk down. Create a series of stepping stones towards your goal. Centre the stones around smaller, more manageable goals, so that you will be able to see progress. It may be that you change your direction en route and that is OK too. Whatever you do, if your goals are large, ignore the "nay" sayers. There will be many who will try to dissuade you from a large goal. My advice is to follow your passion, no matter how many obstacles they put in your path. The negativity of others is a battle we must all constantly fight. This is especially true concerning our career goals.

—

If your goals are too small, such as just wanting to get a job, start looking at the bigger picture. Where do you want to see yourself when you are 30, 40, 50, or 60 years old?

What job can at least move you forward in that direction?

To be, or not to be, an Entrepreneur

There are quizzes and tests to determine if you would be successful managing a business.

Some of them can be found online, and some of them are in your job coach's tool box.

Apart from various skills, you also need to ascertain that you have the right values, needs and personal traits to succeed. If you are interested, talk to your job coach about entrepreneurial programs and services. There are several out there.

Summary

There are many methods of testing and vocational evaluation tools available. Work with your job coach to see which ones best suit your situation. If your job coach does not see the merit of having a career goal, but merely wants to place you in employment, then my advice is to seek out another employment counselor. Good counselors have many tools and techniques to assist you with your discovery phase.

CHAPTER FOUR

RESUMES

Your resume is a vital tool. Compare your resume to a lottery ticket. There are those tickets that only cost a buck, or two, but the chances of winning are one in a million. Then there are those lottery tickets that cost $100, but your chances of winning increase dramatically to about one in five odds. Most resumes fall in to the regular lottery type category and are quickly tossed in to blue recycle bins. I have seen many a human resources manager having a good chuckle out of some of them first, before tossing them in. Job coaches, like myself, keep them as examples of what not to do. You want your resume to be the latter kind of lottery ticket, with high odds of getting you an interview.

Until you know your goals, you are not ready to create your resume.

There is a reason for them being quickly discarded. The most important part of your resume is your objective. I'm sure you have all heard by now that hiring managers generally spend 5 to 30 seconds reviewing your resume, unless they have a good reason to read more. The first thing they do is to check out your objective. If it fits with positions that they are hoping to fill, then they will read more. It needs to be concise, direct and clear.

To quote one Human Resources Manager that I sat with; "Look at this resume. This person expects me to read through it and then figure out what I think they should do." Glancing at the hundreds, yes hundreds, on her desk, I knew that that wasn't very likely to occur.

Some of the more recent resume books suggest that an objective is no longer necessary.

If you decide to go without an objective, start with a brief summary or mission statement that state your goal.

Looks

Stick to plain fonts such as Arial, or Times New Roman. Use white paper with black type, unless you are applying for a creative, or graphic arts position. Plain and simple = easy to read.

Keep it to one or two pages maximum by using only the most recent, and / or, most relevant information. When you are screening through resumes, there is nothing as daunting as a huge stack of pages which relate to only one person. Your resume is not a biography. It is just an introduction to get you an interview.

The exceptions to the two page maximum are for:

- Teachers and academia
- Engineers and Project Managers
- IT professionals

Less is more

A resume is not just a dry boring list of the jobs and duties you have held. That is backwards thinking. Mention the skills that you would like to offer and how they would fit with the position mentioned in your objective. Everything on the page, or pages, should fit with the objective. If it does not, then it is not relevant and should be removed. I'll use myself for example. As a job coach, I am sure you would be interested in my qualifications and experience in that field. But, of course, I have worked in other fields—literally! For four years I worked in agriculture in a dairy farming community. I can still recognize strong hips and a good udder when I see them! But, do you care about that, if you are hiring me as a job coach? I hope not! Therefore, it is not on my resume.

The average person has approximately 150 transferable skills. So, keep your list to the most pertinent ones for your objective. If you feel you are straying from the main point, then remember my udder story. Check out the McMaster University website, under career services, entitled getting ready to write.

Remember that one of the most frequent mistakes is leaving out either your e-mail address, or your phone number. Also common are silly mistakes like typos and incorrect grammar. Have someone else review it, before you fly it off to the employer. Not your room mate, grandmother, or brother-in-law. Choose a professional job coach, human resources staff or hiring manager.

Profile

Once you have your heading set up and your objective stated, it is time to set up a section of highlights, qualifications, or profile. This is where you need to get creative. Think about your values, personality traits, skills, experience and education. What is it that sets you apart from the crowd? What special qualities and qualifications do you have that relate directly to your objective?

Most prospective candidates put this section in bullet form, so that it is easy for an employer to read. The general rule of thumb is to have five to ten statements. Base your statements on yourself and what is required in the position.

Do not repeat yourself. I have seen profile sections that resemble the following:

- Strong interpersonal skills
- Strong computer skills
- Strong customer service skills

Change it up a bit each time so that it is interesting to read, such as:

- Exceptional interpersonal skills
- Ability to build rapport easily with customers
- Excellent computer skills

When it comes to computer skills, be specific. I have had people tell me that they have excellent computer skills, when in fact, they knew only one software program. List exactly which ones you are comfortable working with. If you really are exceptional in your computer ability, then give it a separate heading to showcase it. This could also apply for other positions, such as highlighting customer service, medical knowledge, etc., with separate headings.

Quantify and qualify your statements, if possible.

For example:

- Five years experience in training
- Increased sales by 5% in first year
- Supervised a staff of 25

Order

OK. So, we have a heading, an objective and a list of highlights.

What comes next?

Here is where your resume becomes individualized.

What is most recent? Is it education, or experience? Which is more important to the position?

If it is your experience, then list your work history next. Keep it brief! The parts the hiring manager finds of interest, will be the items they question you on in your interview. If you were to put it all in a resume, what would be left to discuss?

Volunteer Experience

If you have valuable volunteer experience, I would include it on page two, if you have enough space. Employers are usually impressed that you have given your time, and expertise, to your community.

Hobbies/Interests

To include, or not to include hobbies?

That is the question!

This is really a matter of personal choice. If your hobbies are in any way relevant to your career goal, then I would recommend including them. If your hobbies have no relevance, then you might reconsider.

Warning—Do not list any pastimes that may brand you as unsuitable for the position.

References

It is wise to put a short statement concerning references at the end of your resume. An employer may otherwise assume that you do not have any.

Electronic Resumes

Once you are set up with a regular resume, it is a good idea to return to the drawing board and create an electronic resume. These are the ugly ducklings of the resume world. They need to be in a plain text format with no bold letters or underlining. This is because it makes it easier for the computer to read them that way. The idea of an electronic resume is completely different than your regular one, so it is advisable not to just convert it. Remember that this document is read by a machine that is programmed to pick out "key" words that the employer has plugged in. So, it not only needs to look ugly, it needs to be boring! The more ways / words you can use to repeat the same type of information, the better.

For information on creating a great e resume go to:

www.susanireland.com
or, e Resumes book by Susan Britton Whitcomb and Pat Kendall
Excellent resume books, for concrete examples of paper resumes, I would recommend reviewing:
Resume Magic by Susan Britton Whitcomb
The Resume Catalog: 200 Damn Good Examples by Yana Parker
Blue Collar Resumes by Steven Provenzana
Blue Collar and Beyond by Yana Parker
You do not necessarily have to purchase these books, as most employment resource centres carry them.

CHAPTER FIVE

COVER LETTERS

Send not your resume naked out in to the world. Your cover letter is another vital tool in your job search. Many employers have told me that they won't even look at a resume, unless it arrives with a cover letter. When there are the hundreds on their desk, a cover letter attached can be a way of screening out a whole pile of less enthusiastic job seekers.

Your cover letter should consist of three parts.

1. Introduction
2. Sales pitch
3. Wrap up

In your introduction, make it very clear what position you are asking to be considered for. Avoid wishy-washy statements like, "A position with your company where I can utilize my skills and abilities, blah, blah." Employers are not going to take the time to figure out what you want from them. Also, the position you are seeking is for them to utilize your skills and abilities, not the other way around. When job searching, you are selling yourself, in return for what the employer is offering.

Make sure you know what you want your employer to offer you. Are you looking for a start in a new career? Are you hoping for a good salary? Are benefits important? Do you need to value the work that you do? Go back and review your career testing. Getting a job is like buying a home. It is a two-way street. The employer has needs to fill, and so do you. So, you know what you are prepared to offer and you need to determine if the employer's offer fits your needs. The employer's advertisement usually gives an outline of their offer and your cover letter is explaining your counter offer.

Paragraph two, or your sales pitch, is where you showcase what sets you apart from the crowd. Imagine it as your reply to, "So, why should we hire you?" To prepare this section, you will need to research the company in depth. Make sure that you really are a good fit, so that you don't waste the employer's time, and your own time.

Construct your cover letter to be different from your resume, using diverse language and skill sets. An employer does not want to see that you have copied words directly off of their advertisement either. They are probably not in the market for a parrot! Come up with something fresh and energetic, to capture their imagination.

Repetitiveness is boring.

Repetitiveness is boring.

I think you can see my point here.

No one wants to hire someone who is boring and who lacks imagination. Even general labour positions can be improved by front line staff with innovative ideas to enhance the way that work is processed. Creativity is a key commodity.

For your wrap up, thank them for taking the time to review your documents. Depending upon your personality type, either request that they contact you for a face to face meeting, or let them know that you will be following up with them. If you state a date that you will be following up with them, make sure you stick to it like glue, so they can see that you follow through on assignments.

If you have asked them to contact you, it is still advisable to give them a call in a few days to make sure that your cover letter and resume have been received. That way, if your documents have gone astray, either physically, or electronically, you can resend them. By asking the hiring manager to look for them, you have now brought them to his/her attention, rather than leaving them languishing in the heap. If, on the other hand, they specify "no phone calls please", then do not call. They may assume that you can not adhere to directions.

Style

It is quite acceptable to prepare your cover letter in either paragraph, or point, form. Use whichever better suits your personality type and the position you are applying for. There is no right, or wrong, to either format. Go with your gut and use your own personal style.

There are dozens of books with cover letter examples in them. I would recommend reviewing:

Cover Letter Magic by Wendy S. Enelowt and Louise Kursmark

CHAPTER SIX

JOB SEARCHING

To be successful in your job search, you need to spend a great deal of time doing it. Contrary to some people's beliefs, a job is not going to knock on your door and announce, "Here I am." You are required to do a lot of leg work.

Your research needs to be in three stages.

1. Know yourself and what you are looking for.
2. Research the labour market to see if those type of positions are available and where.
3. Sell yourself through various job search methods such as networking, cold calling, walking in and submitting your documents online.

These steps must be done in the correct order, or you will dramatically reduce your chances of getting hired.

Remember to tap in to the hidden job market through your networking efforts.

See Chapter Eight for tips on this.

Warning. The six most common job search mistakes, according to the McMaster University Counseling Centre are:

1. Not knowing what you have to offer.
2. Not taking an active approach.
3. Not maintaining a positive attitude.
4. Not thinking from an employer's perspective.

---

5. Not following up properly.
6. Remaining alone.

Solution. Working with an organization, or individual job coach, will help you with all of the above.

For blue collar positions and entry level jobs, I would recommend walking in. Believe it or not, you have a one in five chance that they are hiring at that time. If you are a betting person, you know that those are pretty good odds! Walking in gives you a chance to look around and pick up on the atmosphere, dress code, and culture of that particular workplace. It provides you with vital clues that you can utilize in an interview.

The golden rule when walking in is to never come away empty handed. If you have requested to see the hiring manager, or HR official, and they are busy, ask for their contact information so you can send your documents directly to their attention.

Warning. Do not randomly leave documents with receptionists or other staff. Your odds there are that they will be hurriedly blue binned!

For white collar workers, professionals and academia, the application rules change. You will better succeed by having exceptionally well prepared documents and by utilizing networking and online research. For IT professionals, engineers, and academia, even the length of your resume is different. You are not restricted to the one or two page norm. Your resume must include much more detail on computer applications, papers published, and achievements. These employers are looking for results oriented individuals and need you to quantify, or measure, your knowledge.

Job Fairs

Job Fairs are a good way of interacting directly with employers. Some job fairs are specifically for job seekers with disabilities. The employers that attend these venues are often equity employers who have a quota to fill of the federally designated Canadian groups which are currently:

1. Persons with disabilities
2. Visible Minorities
3. Women
4. Aboriginals

With these employers, you are at an advantage to be a person with a disability. Because they are obligated to fill positions with these target groups, they are really there to sell themselves and their company to you.

Warning: Job fairs can be very crowded places that are difficult to maneuver. Behind their wonderful display units, most employers keep two piles of resumes. The huge pile is likely to be their discard, or blue box set. The small pile is of the ones who have impressed them face to face, and who they are actually going to look at.

Solution: Go prepared with a short elevator speech, so that they will select your resume for the review pile. Dress for success. Find out which employers are going to be at the fair. Research the companies ahead of time. Know which ones are your key targets, and head for them first, rather than just going around the whole room in order. It doesn't take long for huge line ups to develop and you want to make sure you can get to meet with the ones who matter most to you. Have a few key questions to ask them. That will set you apart from the crowd, and give them the opportunity to showcase their business.

If approaching employers is difficult for you, remember, practice makes perfect. The more hiring managers you talk to, the easier it becomes and the more relaxed you appear.

One of the most important things you can do is to radiate energy and enthusiasm!

Second Warning: Do not limit yourself to only job fairs for persons with disabilities. There are many employers out there who may not be equity employers, but that are true equal opportunity employers.

Keeping Organized

Use whatever system works best for you, to keep yourself organized during your job search. You will need a method of listing which companies, or organizations, you have applied to. That way, should you be fortunate enough to get a call from them, you will recognize who they are and not fumble the ball. Keep your resume, paper and pencils, or some form of note taker, by the telephone. Many employers use your resume as a template for a prescreening, telephone interview. They are likely to ask you questions based on the qualifications listed on your resume. Be well prepared with answers.

For example: If on your resume, it says you are highly organized, get ready with an example of why this is the case. Perhaps use your method of organizing your job search as an example!

Volunteer Work

Volunteering is a great way to get introduced to an employer, or organization. This is especially true if you are career changing, or have been out of the workforce for an extended period. Volunteering allows you to prove yourself to the employer, before they make a commitment to hire you. It also allows you to gain valuable work experience. For those of you who are new to Canada and are tired of hearing the phrase, "You don't have any Canadian experience," this is your answer. Remember, work is work, whether it is paid for, or done on a volunteer basis.

Volunteering also allows you the opportunity to network. By meeting people where you volunteer, you are expanding your network of connections. There are also people working there with you who could provide you with a reference. Volunteering allows to try your hand at a different job, without committing to the long haul. You may find you love the work and you may find that it wasn't quite what you imagined. If you are new to your disability and are uncertain how it may impact you in the workplace, volunteering is a great way to find out.

I could use another client story here, but I'm going to tell you one of my own. At one point in my life I moved to a small rural community where I didn't know anyone. I decided to throw myself in to volunteer work for the first couple of years. I made some very valuable connections, among the community go getters, who were also giving their time to volunteer work. Through this new branch of my network, a job opportunity presented itself. It was not an advertised position. I felt that I was not qualified for it since it involved agriculture, which I had no formal education in and very little experience. However, I was encouraged to apply and managed to secure the position. When I asked them why they hired me, the reply was that they knew I would successfully run the project because of my reputation in the community through my volunteer management experience.

If you have a particular charity, or passion, that is close to your heart I would advise you to volunteer in that sector, if possible. If nothing springs to mind, then here are a few websites for your research:

Charity Village *www.charityvillage.com*
Volunteers *www.volunteer.ca*
Global Volunteer *www.globalvolunteers.org*
Youth Cyberstation *www.pch.gc.ca/cyberstation*
Head Hunters *www.headhunters.com*

Research

The bulk of your work should be in research, making sure you know what you want and then finding organizations that fit that model.

Client B was new to the community from outside of the province and did not know local people to network with. She attended my employment workshops and set to work immediately researching. Her field of expertise was as a health care administrator.

She went laboriously through the book of service providers and read their brief bios. This phase of her research took several weeks before she chose what she felt were her top five choices. She spent a lot of time on more in-depth research of those five. Then she tailored five very individual cover letters and resumes and submitted them. None of the organizations were currently advertising any openings. Of the five employers, three invited her to an interview. One of them was so impressed with her knowledge of their organization, and the business in general, that they created a position for her. She worked with them for two years on a contract basis. Of course, during the two years, she had utilized part of her time by creating a network within the industry and she had no trouble moving on to another project.

Time Lines

When you come across an advertised position that has an application deadline date, do not assume that it is inflexible.

Your best advantage is to apply early on in the process, rather than wait until the deadline. One reason is that hiring managers are human; well usually! They often naturally start to look at documents as they trickle in. In many cases they have short listed five, or more, strong candidates from the early birds and may not even be looking at others that are submitted after that date. I can guarantee you that it happens. I know of one case, where the employer had actually made a job offer, before their deadline date.

Yes, I know that this may not be fair. But again, we can not change the world. What you can do is make sure your application is submitted early, rather than late.

On the other side of the coin, the deadline may have passed and they may not have what they consider to be strong candidates. If you come across a position that you feel is your ultimate dream job, but the deadline is passed, give them a call in any case. Let them know how interested you are in the role, that you realize the published deadline is passed, but you are wondering if they would still accept a submission from you. What have you got to lose, in any case? Just a few minutes for a phone call. Be sure to speak to the person in charge of the hiring, not a receptionist.

CHAPTER SEVEN

NETWORKING

Networking is so vital to your career path, that I have included a whole chapter on it.

In a job search scenario, networking can provide you with valuable information and, if you are successful, that coveted inside job lead.

Why is that insider's lead so important, compared to just doing the regular job search stuff, like looking for postings on the internet? First of all, you are eliminating most, if not all, of the competition. If it isn't advertised, then there shouldn't be many people applying for it. Inside referrals are popular with hiring managers because they save them a huge amount of time, and money, by short circuiting the hiring process.

How can you successfully network?

Make the most of social gatherings, talk to people in libraries, resource centres, online, anywhere! Start by listing all of the people you can network with. Remember to include everyone you associate with. Utilize past co-workers, teachers, friends, people on your email list etc. Be sure to network with people in public.

What about in person?

Dress for success everywhere you go when you are in the market for that plum job.

Have a business card ready to hand out. It only needs your contact information and a about three lines of qualifications. The advantage of the business card is that it is easy for your contact to slip in a pocket, wallet, or

---

purse. If you are attending a social function, they may not want to tuck away wads of resumes.

Go for quality—not quantity. Stick to your top three selling points.

What should you send out electronically and on large job search internet sites?

Send out a resume with an email address only, as contact information, for your own security. Literally, thousands of people visit large job search sites. One of them could be an ax murderer!

Other methods of Networking

Attend professional events.
Go to job fairs.
Join a structured networking group online.

Structured Networking Groups

These can range from a Job Club, where you share job leads, to electronic social groups. The advantage of an online group is that it allows you access to a large number of like minded individuals. For example: in 2009, *www.linkedin.com* had 38 million members from over 200 countries. The disadvantage is that you need to be careful of your privacy, as you are getting huge exposure.

Face to Face Scenarios

Here are a few real life examples:

Client C wanted to get an introduction to a hiring manager at a company where he hoped to work. Despite several phone call attempts, and a visit with the dragon at the front desk, he was getting nowhere. Being a smoker, he decided, on exiting the building, to join in with a group of workers indulging in a smoke break. He struck up a conversation with an employee and won himself an introduction. Bingo! Dragon lady side stepped.

Client D needed to relocate to where she had grown up. She decided to go and research jobs and a place to live in the area. Although now middle aged, Client D ran in to one of her high school chums from many years ago, in a coffee shop. They talked about life in general and she utilized the networking opportunity to enquire if the friend knew of any available jobs. The friend was running her own business and was in dire need of someone with Client D's qualifications. Bingo! Job secured.

Client E was looking for a job in Toronto. She contacted everyone she could think of to get the word out. One of her telephone calls was to a friend in Calgary. What possible use could that be, when she was looking in Toronto? Well, the friend had another friend, who worked in Toronto and knew of an upcoming opening with her employer. Bingo! Contact secured and interview followed.

Client F had attended one of my workshops where I drone on about networking possibilities. One of the things I always recommend, is to utilize your electronic friends on your email list, Facebook site, etc. During the lunch break, she flew out a quick note to everyone on her email list. The message was short and to the point, stating that she was in the market for the following type of employment opportunity. During the coffee break in the afternoon class, she checked her email inbox. There were 5 messages regarding unadvertised job opportunities. Bingo! Five leads to follow up on, for five minutes work.

For myself, I network everywhere. Yes, everywhere from ladies toilets, elevators, grocery store lines, ad infinitum. My favourite place? Weddings. Absolutely. Everyone is in a good mood and there is always time to chat at a reception. Which brings me to Client G.

Client G was looking for a start in the construction trade. At a wedding I attended, the bride's father owned a successful building business. Needless to say, I utilized the networking opportunity and—you guessed it. Bingo! Job secured. Wedding on Saturday. Client employed the following Monday morning.

I have a lot more networking stories available, but I think I have made my point. So here are a few tips:

Networking Tips:

Create business cards so that you are ready to take advantage of any chance meetings. If you are not super computer savvy, you can use a template on Microsoft Word.

Consider email contacts, personal contacts, volunteer contacts and social networking groups.

* Continually update and expand your networks.

Keep extra resumes that have only your email address listed for contact purposes. This works well if you are concerned about privacy for electronic or social networking.

Examples of Social networking groups:

Pink Slip parties—*http://thepinkslipparty.eventbrite.com*
Cost is approximately $20 per evening

Happen Inc.—for mid to senior level executives in Toronto for weekly meeting and social networking online *http://www.happen.ca* FREE
www.Myspace.com
www.Facebook.com
www.Linkedin.com

Elevator Speech

This is your two minute blurb on what you are looking for and why you are so perfect for that role.

Focus on quality not quantity.

Check out: *www.creativekeys.net/PowerfulPresentations/srticle1024.html*
www.quintcareers.com/elevator_speech_dos-donts.html
www.expressionsofexcellence.com/sample_elevator.html

Just like your resume, less is more. Don't bore them. People hate to waste time, especially these days, when time is such a priceless commodity. Your elevator speech is just to pique their curiosity. If they are seriously interested, they will ask you for more.

CHAPTER EIGHT

INTERVIEWS

Well, there have been dozens of books about interview skills, how to ace those tricky answers etc., but I'd like to put a different spin on this topic.

Interviews, like resumes, are constantly changing format and style. The most recent popular format is known as the Behavioral Interview. There is an abundance of material on the market about this and there are dozens of agencies that train people in this style. Therefore, I am not going to beat a dead horse. Besides, in my opinion, I think the behavioral interview is an overworked donkey, shortly to be replaced by a car! A behavioral interview merely demonstrates that you can remember your pre-rehearsed answers to some very predictable questions. It's about as exciting as balancing your cheque book. You stick to the correct method and your bank balance will be correct.

My apologies to all of you budding accountants!

Am I crazy? It's always possible. So, why do I think that?

The unemployed job seeker, who is proactive in their job search, knows how to ace these interviews. They have been trained. In any case, it doesn't really tell the employer much about their candidate. It is backwards thinking. It assumes that because you have reacted a certain way in the past, you are likely to react that way in the future. But humans are evolving beings. By and large we learn from our mistakes and don't always act the way we may have in the past. We should learn and grow. I know I have. Haven't you?

My other big concern about behavioral type interviews is that almost anyone can learn to do well at them, regardless of whether or not they would be a good fit for the job. During my many years of employment, in various sectors, I have come across numerous co-workers who aced their interviews, but were hopeless at their jobs. They probably got there through answering practiced behavioral questions.

So, what is a good way to approach an upcoming interview? Speaking from personal experience, the last two interviews I had, were not behavioral at all. Both included an on the spot demonstration of skills in front of the prospective employers eyes. So they were a showcase of my abilities. The other parts of the interview were mainly conversational, and of course, I had several questions prepared for those employers. During the preparation for writing this book, I questioned a lot of other people about their recent interview experiences. Most of them had skills based, conversational type interviews. Some still had behavioral ones and a few had some psychological questions thrown in, for good measure.

Note Taking

On a little aside, I would like to mention note taking, as it is something I get questioned about a lot. My advice is always:

If you have a learning disability, memory loss, or any other reason why note taking is essential to you, then, by all means request to take notes at an interview.

If you do not need them, however, I would strongly advise you not to use them.

An employer will be far more impressed if you can engage him/her in informed conversation than if you are constantly looking down and taking copious notes.

This is especially true if you are applying for a job where adaptability is a key factor. Taking numerous notes might suggest that you are unable to think on your feet and respond quickly in a problem solving situation. You may also be missing out on some of their key body language if you are busy scribbling away. I have actually known people who have attended presentations, taken bounteous notes, and not had an inkling afterwards what the presentation was about. They were too busy jotting things down to pay attention and in their jotting they were always one, or two, steps behind the presenter.

An employer will be more impressed if you bring fresh ideas of your own, than merely copy down what they are already doing.

Preparation

You can never prepare too much for an interview. So, start by doing your homework.

What are the employer's mission statement, mandate and values? Do they match reasonably with yours? Are you comfortable with the organization's future goals?

If so; why? The answer to this question is the key to your good fit and suitability for the position.

If you are a methodical person, make a two sided list of your needs and what you perceive, through research, to be your employer's needs.

Here are a few things you might wish to consider. Your list may be much longer, depending upon your personal wants and needs.

To value what I do / just work for a paycheque
This much $ to survive
Within this distance of my home
With flexibility / with set rules and strict guidelines
With this type of manager
With a team / on my own
Up front with customers and the public / behind the scenes
With traveling / with no traveling involved
Routine / challenging
To receive recognition
Methodical and repetitive work / constantly evolving and changing role

Here are a few basic ideas for the employer's perceived needs. Again, the list could vary considerably, so don't rely on these solely.

An employee who is:

Reliable / flexible
Able to follow directions / able to work independently to solve problems
Who can work shifts
Who will remain in the position long term / who will accept a short tern contract
Who is willing to move laterally within the organization
Who is well qualified and experienced
Who is entry level, but willing to learn through the company training programs

At some point in the interview, let them know how you can add value to their team, their bottom line, or any aspect of their business.

If you attend a skills based interview, make sure that what is listed on your resume, is correct. For example, if you say you can keyboard 60 words per minute, in a skills based interview, you might be required to demonstrate your keyboarding skills. Sixty words per minute does not just mean speed, it means accuracy. If you are applying for a customer service role, you may be required to demonstrate your use of tone and language. For example, banks who hire telephone customer service reps, actually test them on imagined scenarios with customers.

Interviewers

Not all interviewers are experts. In fact, some of them fall in to that "Ugly" category.

While I was writing this book, Client H had an interview. He was looking for a position as bar tender, waiter and banquet preparer in a large hotel. He had undergone a very successful first interview with the hotel manager. The interview was a conversational one, verifying that my client knew his products and customer service. His second interview was with a newly hired Food and Beverage Manager. The hotel was an upscale, boutique style hotel, mainly frequented by middle aged, middle class, patrons. The new manager conducted a behavioural type interview, sticking closely to her pre arranged questions and making copious notes. She had no time to gauge the body language, or enthusiasm of my client. When it was his turn to question her, he hoped to demonstrate his extensive knowledge of food and wines. Unfortunately, the interviewer knew little about food and nothing about wines. Nothing! A food and **Beverage** Manager! So, he switched to asking her about the hotel. Her response was to say that she had only been there a couple of days and could not answer any of his questions. SCARY! To think she is being paid for this, and probably a decent salary too! Naturally my client was quite upset that he had not performed well in the interview. My response was: "Do you really want to work for a manager that knows nothing about the business?" I rest my case.

The question everyone hates

So, what would you say is your weakness?
Of course, you don't want to have a weakness, because you want them hire you, right? But, this is almost a guaranteed question. The way I see it, you have three ways of responding.

1. You take an actual strength and word it as though you are revealing a weakness.

   For example, you could say that you have an abhorrence to clutter and you need to take the time to organize your work station each day before

---

starting. You would follow that up by saying that you usually arrive early because of this weakness. The employer will be impressed by your dedication and see your fussiness as a strength, rather than a fault.

2. You take an actual weakness, but show how you are going to take corrective action because of it.

   For example, you may not be completely educationally qualified for the profession you are entering, but money is tight and you need a start. Explain to the prospective employer how you have arranged to attend evening classes, or are completing your studies online by such and such a date.

3. Just be honest.

I am a very straightforward person. If an employer wants someone who is extremely tactful and treads carefully around issues, then they do not want to hire me. For my answer, I let them know that I am a very plain speaking person and some clients may be offended by the fact that I am not afraid to tell them my opinion about why they are not getting hired. I have developed this style from working with challenging groups such as marginal youth.

References

Be sure to have a typed up sheet of references ready to hand over at an interview. The general rule is to have a list of three. Some employers may ask for more to be provided. By having a list for them, you are demonstrating that you are organized, well prepared for your interview, and eager for the position.

If you are unable to come up with three work references, then do a mix and match of professional references and personal ones. Do not use your family.

Warning: Ensure you have contacted all of your listed references ahead of time and that they are ready to vouch for you. If they sound non-committal, then try to use another person. Some companies will only state that you have worked for them and when. In those cases, shoot for a co-worker who can verify your skills and personal qualities. This needs to be completed, before you go to an interview. In one of my own experiences, my prospective employer was telephoning my references, while I was engaged in a testing phase of the interview.

I have chosen not to include example interview questions here, because it really depends on the type of position you are applying for, so it could be a whole other book. If you are very interested in reviewing questions, check out:

Answering Tough Interview Questions for Dummies by Rob Young
Knock En Dead—Interview Questions by Martin Yate

Chapter Nine

SECONDARY DISABILITIES / DEPRESSION

This may be a short chapter, but it is one that I feel needs touching upon.

The U.S. Department of Health and Human Services, for the first time in its' study Healthy People 2010, has included a chapter on disability. One of their directives was to attempt to eliminate "the disparities in employment rates between working-aged adults with and without disabilities." Part of the identified problem was that there are often secondary disabilities, or significant health factors, that impact working. There were several mentioned, one of which was depression, arising from a major lifestyle change due to your primary disability. Of course, a form of depression could also be your primary disability.

When dealing with depression, I always refer to my main motto in life which is, "Assumptions are the mother of all mistakes." Not everyone who has a disability, suffers from depression. Not everyone who suffers from depression, is disabled by it. It is a fine line to be walked very carefully. If you are unsure whether you may be suffering from depression as a secondary disability, then my advice is to consult an expert.

When you are in the midst of a career change and are job searching, there is a huge range of emotions that you may well experience. Depression is a very real risk factor for all of us. The following study looks at ways to shift from a negative perspective to a positive one. The study was one of Canada Employment Centre users by Amundsen and Borgen, in *The Experience of Unemployment*.

Shifts from Negative to Positive

1. Job Rejection → Supportive Family/Friends
2. Financial Pressure → Temporary Work
3. Family Problems → Thinking Positively
4. Job Search Activities → Job Support Group
5. Thinking Negatively → Plan/Acceptance for Re-training
6. Future Unknown or Negative → Volunteer Work
7. Lack of English / Training in Country of Origin → Taking Courses
8. Watching T.V. → Engaged in job search
9. Drinking/Smoking → Physical Exercise
10. Stress → Vacation

When you take action, you change your mindset to a more positive one, because you have become unstuck from stagnation. Imagine your barriers as brick walls. If you can not get over that wall, then you must find a way around it, or even dig under it if you have to, to move forward towards your goal.

There are many stress relieving exercises and methods that you can use when you are in the midst of job searching, or any life transition. There are dozens of other books, brochures and websites on this topic. Here is one website example:

http://www.stress-relief-exercises.com

CHAPTER TEN

RECENT DISABILITIES

Job searching is a tough job. You can expect to experience a roller coaster of emotions.

Frustration, exhaustion, elation, and disappointment, are just a few of them. It is much harder than actually working, and is no place for the unsure, uncommitted, or half hearted.

For those of you who are new to a disability

1. Allow yourself time to grieve. If you have lost some mobility, some vision, your previous job, or anything at all, then you have the right to grieve. Take your time. Come to terms with your new reality. Remember, you are still the same person. Reflect on your accomplishments.

When I was unable to work full time, in a structured environment, my health practitioner warned me that it would take three to four months to adjust. I thought he was being silly. It took me four months, almost to the day, and a lot of soul searching, before I could consider moving on and working differently. It may take you less. It may take you longer. Give yourself the time **you** need to adjust.

Concentrate on what you can still do, not on what you can not do. Consult with experts on your particular disability. Join a support group. Find out about others, with your type of disability, who are succeeding. Rely heavily on your friends and those that Oprah Winfrey calls your "bone marrow people."

Accept that you may lose some of your confidence at the start of the process. With each stage of progression, where you are moving forward, such as joining a training program or working with an individual job coach, your confidence will start to reestablish itself.

2. Make sure you are **ready** for your job searching task. You will need to be stable, emotionally and in your physical surroundings. If you are still living in transition due to a recent disability, it is not a great time to start job searching. You will require a place to prepare yourself for interviews, an e-mail account and a telephone. If you can not afford a computer, then you might join a local library, or job search club, and utilize theirs. If you can not afford a telephone, then get a pay as you go cell phone for the time being.

Emotionally, make sure that your grieving process is over. Once your have acceptance of your new parameters, then you are ready to move forward. The onus for job searching is on you, so make sure you are ready to commit your time and effort to the task ahead.

Note: If you are hooked up with a job coach, you can be sure they will be gauging whether you are READY, WILLING and ABLE to work with them.

3. Know your disability inside out. Only you know what accommodations you will require on the job. If you do not, then consult with an expert. Many non-profit agencies can assist you with this advice for free. There are various tools and technologies out there to improve working and living conditions. For further information on software and technology that may be of help to you, drop me an e-mail and I will respond.

Remember: Even other persons with the same disability as yourself, may be affected entirely differently. Each person is unique, and so is their disability.

CHAPTER ELEVEN

HOORAY I'M HIRED!

Keep your employer informed on any changes with your disability, in terms of tools that you need to succeed. Hiding your disability is the worst case scenario. I have listened to many tales of grief, where bosses have been cruel and jobs have been lost, due to an unrevealed disability, or medical condition. Because you have been "fired", or let go, it will add further to your loss of self esteem and personal worth.

Remember, all employment is good experience. Even employment situations that you have disliked intensely, have taught you what to avoid in your future career path. Therefore, if valuable lessons have been learned, then that difficult employment situation was not wasted.

There are no set rules on disclosure. It is a question of what works best for you. If you are unsure on how to best disclose your disability to a prospective employer, then seek professional advice. My only counsel here is to make sure, at some point in the hiring process that you do disclose. Not disclosing at all is tantamount to deceiving an employer and they may view you as being untrustworthy in the future. Discuss what might be best for you, as a unique individual, with your job coach.

If job maintenance has been a concern of yours, then you need to address it with your job coach before you are re-employed. Continually losing positions can be very demoralizing and may affect your self esteem. Work with your coach to identify employer expectations and see where you may be falling short.

Hopefully your new job is smooth sailing. If you find you are having any difficulties, because of your disability, or the terminology used around you, check out the following link which is entitled "A Way With Words."

---

www.hrsdc.gc.ca/en/disability_issues/reports/way_with_words/index.shtml

Remember, you have a legal right to be accommodated in the workplace unless it is deemed to cause undo hardship to the employer.

Chapter Twelve

SUMMING IT ALL UP

1. Do not expect your job coach to do everything for you. You must be your own career manager and play an active role in your career direction.

   The employer should be hiring YOU, not your job coach. If your coach has done everything to get you that job, without effort on your part, then the employer is hiring the wrong man. Or woman. If your job coach does all of your cold calling and networking, how are you demonstrating your enthusiasm and initiative? Here is a quote from What Color is Your Parachute, by Richard Bolles, which is considered to be the Bible of Job searching for most Employment Specialists: "Realize That the Employer Thinks the Way You Are Doing Your Job-Hunt Is the Way You Will Do the Job".
   Check out *www.jobhuntersbible.com*

2. Have clear cut goals. Where do you want to be in 5 years time? If you can't obtain your ideal job at the present time, at least try to find a position that will move you one stepping stone closer to your goal. At one point in my career when I was between contracts, I worked in a convenience store. The experience was very valuable in getting to know about that type of work and it was still interacting with the public on a daily basis, so continued to build on my interpersonal skills.

3. Don't let family members, or well meaning friends, coerce you in to joining a program, or job searching. If I had a penny for all of the prospective clients who ended up in tears, because their wife, partner, grandmother, sister-in-law etc., sent them to me, I would be a very rich woman indeed. Only you know when you are ready.

---

4. Consider future trends of employment. The world of work is rapidly changing and evolving, due to many factors, the most dominant of which is technology. Whatever your personality type, you must learn to embrace change, or you will be left behind. Employers are looking for employees who are adaptable, life long learners, flexible on job descriptions and enthusiastic about moving laterally within the organization. Be open to new ways of working, such as from a home office, as parameters and priorities change.

5. How badly do you want to work? Be prepared to accept contract positions. Be prepared to work on a volunteer basis, to get yourself known. Be prepared to start out part time. All these are particularly important if you are career changing, or re-entering the workforce after an extended absence.

6. There is no shame in any work you choose to do. Some people have a strong vocation and develop a career for themselves that matches their innermost urgings. Others chose simply to work for money and use their free time to enjoy hobbies, express themselves artistically, and enjoy life. Either way is fine. It must be what is right for you. This is where your career tests become important as your starting point.

7. Job coaches and employment specialists are just that, *employment* specialists. We are only experts in the field of employment. Many of my clients wish that the market was better, employers were more empathetic, life was fair, the world was a better place, etc. I let them know that, as much as I might like to change things like world hunger, I have no control over those things. The only thing I can do is to try and give them the best possible chance of getting hired and enjoying their work.

8. A good job coach's purpose in life is to make you, the job seeker, independent of them. Just like a parent teaches their child the rules of life and then sets them free to make of them what they will, so does an employment counselor. Your ultimate aim should be to learn to job search on your own, so that you no longer need us. If that is accomplished, then we have both succeeded.

9. Know your labour market. There is no point in deciding to become a hair dresser in a town that already has too many hairdressers! Your employment specialist should be able to show you where to conduct your research. Service Canada also has statistics on salaries and positions on their website.

10. In all cases where I have recommended books, or websites, be sure to research your own. You will need to use the information that best fits your career goal. My recommendations are guidelines only.

About The Author

Judith is a private consultant with a fee for service practice. Her business encompasses facilitating workshops for client groups, counseling individuals and team building for organizations. She is also available as a motivational speaker at conferences and training sessions. Her business is called Canada Career Coach.

I would love to hear your views, ideas and criticisms. Please do contact me for suggestions, advice, or just networking at:

Jobcoachjudith@gmail.com

Illustrators

Andre Beaupre is a graphic designer in Montreal. He can be contacted at *andre_beaupre@sympatico.ca*

Bastien Trépanier, is a newly graduate in animated movies from cégep du Vieux-Montréal, in Montreal, Quebec. This is his first official contract as an illustrator. He always had a fascination for cartoon movies, and movies at large. That childhood passion became his goal, and he is still pursuing that dream… He is presently waiting to enter a course (technical degree) in motion pictures and television production.

www.ingramcontent.com/pod-product-compliance
Lightning Source LLC
Chambersburg PA
CBHW021548290526
45784CB00016B/2359

9781465352385